HOMAGE TO
SØREN
KIERKEGAARD

WISEBLOOD BOOKS

Wiseblood Books
P.O. Box 870
Menomonee Falls, WI 53052

Printed in the United States of America

Set in Calluna Typesetting
Cover Design: Amanda Brown

ISBN 13: Paperback: 978-1-951319-41-0

Wiseblood Books

HOMAGE TO
SØREN KIERKEGAARD:

Poems in Memory of
Reverend Ronald Marshall

AN ANTHOLOGY EDITED BY
DANA GIOIA & MARY GRACE MANGANO

WISEBLOOD BOOKS

CONTENTS

POEMS

PREFACE

In early 2013 I received a letter from Reverend Ronald Marshall, a minister and theologian, who was the pastor of the First Lutheran Church of West Seattle. He asked if he could commission me to write a poem about Søren Kierkegaard in honor of the philosopher's bicentennial. He offered a respectable fee and complete freedom for the poem's style and approach.

Marshall introduced himself by declaring his fascination with Kierkegaard, about whose work he had published two books and numerous articles. Later I came to understand that his passion for the Danish philosopher represented a sort of saintly devotion, similar to the intellectual reverence Catholic theologians show Augustine, Thomas Aquinas, or Teresa of Avila. Each year he gave a sermon on the anniversary of Kierkegaard's death. That choice of date struck me as odd until I realized that a saint's death is also his birth into eternal life.

I did not yet know all of these things about Marshall, but his letter made an impression—a generous invitation from a thoughtful clergyman to undertake a worthy project. A poet doesn't often get such letters.

I had, however, to decline the invitation. As I explained to Marshall, I was hopeless at writing occasional poems. I might produce some tolerable verse but not what he desired—a real poem that engaged Kierkegaard. For me, poems came either unbidden or not at all. I suggested another poet well qualified for the project. Marshall replied that he was disappointed but understood my reservations.

I also told Marshall that Kierkegaard remained a challenging figure for me. I had read several of his major books and could recite a conventional summary of his ideas, but he remained a remote and ambiguous thinker. I had never connected—intellectually or emotionally—with the core of his philosophy. I found him more difficult than Kant or Heidegger. My confusion delighted Marshall. As I was to discover, he had begun one of his essays on Kierkegaard by stating, "Reading Kierkegaard can be a bewildering experience." I was one of the readers he described.

Those exchanges happened within a few days of first receiving his invitation. The matter seemed settled. But sometimes you make up your mind and then do just the opposite.

Suddenly I began to think about Kierkegaard. I had to fly to the East Coast, and I pulled my old copy of Walter Lowrie's biography off the shelf and began to reread it on the plane. The book had a profound effect on me. As soon as I got home, I reread *The Concept of Dread* in a state of heightened susceptibility. Then I reread the battered paperback edition of *Fear and Trembling* I had bought in high school.

For the first time, the deep sense of the books became startlingly clear. I felt Kierkegaard's spiritual dilemma in human terms. How could I have been so stupid as to miss it before? He represented the extreme end of Protestant interiority that had been difficult for my Catholic sensibility to understand. Now I finally felt—through all his careful layers of artifice—his alarming power. Then, without warning, a poem came.

A few days later I wrote Marshall and told him that I would have a poem for him. I also said I would decline his commission. The poem had come as a gift to me; I wanted it to be a gift to him. This initiated a short comic struggle. He insisted I accept the fee. I refused. We compromised by sending half the fee to a young writer in financial distress and donating the rest to his parish. The solution delighted us as did our growing friendship—another unexpected gift.

My poem, "Homage to Søren Kierkegaard," moves through the philosopher's odd life counterpointing his biography with his ideas. In that sense it replicates my own path toward understanding his work. That mix of the personal and philosophical pleased Ron. (We were now on first-name terms.) He announced that he planned to have it printed for display in the church lounge adjacent to the chapel. His plan gave me an idea.

I called my friend Michael Peich, the founder of Aralia Press, in West Chester, Pennsylvania. Mike is Lutheran, and I thought the notion of printing the poem might appeal to him. With his usual generosity and enthusiasm, Mike offered to print a letterpress broadside of "Homage to Søren Kierkegaard" and donate most of the small edition to First Lutheran to be sold as a fundraiser. Ron was overjoyed by the unexpected offer. Mike went to work at once to meet the short deadline, and the broadsheet was delivered in time for Ron's annual November 17th bicentennial service and celebration. The broadside was also soon installed next to the small statue of Kierkegaard that Ron had commissioned years earlier.

A few years later I came to Seattle for another event, and Ron invited me to speak at his parish. It was the only time I had the chance to speak to him face to face and to meet his wife, Jane Harty. We spent a happy day together, and the event was sheer pleasure. By then Ron and I had settled into a steady friendship through email. I was always pleased to see his username appear on my screen—*deogloria,* "to the glory of God,"

Ron usually wrote me about poetry. He was an ideal reader of poetry—curious, intelligent, and deeply thoughtful. He was the sort of reader cultural commentators claim no longer exists, a serious and informed non-specialist. He looked to poetry for the same reasons that Wordsworth or Frost would have—wonder, wisdom, and pleasure.

Every few weeks Ron would drop me a letter or note about whomever he was reading—T. S. Eliot, Emily Dickinson, Philip Larkin, Kay Ryan, R. S. Thomas or Robert Bly. If I published an essay or poem, he would send a response. When Bob Dylan won the Nobel Prize, Ron told me his reaction and wanted to know mine. Like many poetry readers, he felt a sense of isolation. There weren't other serious poetry readers in his daily world he could talk to.

His letters were particularly interesting because he usually quoted lines he admired from the poems he mentioned. In the middle of one note, for example, these lines from Dickinson appeared:

Bred as we, among the mountains,
Can the sailor understand
The divine intoxication
Of the first league out from land?

And there were other surprises. He sent me record-
ings of Jane's excellent piano performances—a selection
of Chopin, or Beethoven's song cycle *An die Ferne Geliebte*
done with a young soprano. And each year he sent me his
sermon for Kierkegaard's anniversary, all of them carefully
constructed and searching meditations on redemption
and salvation. These sermons have none of the bland and
sentimental uplift that constitutes most of today's hom-
ilies. They present a stark Christian existentialism that
would unnerve many congregations. Here is one passage:

> What is it like, then, to be gripped by God so we can
> believe in Christ? Kierkegaard thinks that we can
> learn this from the believers in the Bible—noting
> their "quiet, deep God-fearing sorrow that is silent
> before God"—and his word, which is "the one thing
> needful" (KW 18:149). Such moments are well worth
> utilizing—by calling on God for help (Acts 2:21)! And
> that sorrow, which is deep and silent before God, is
> precisely over our sin. And because this silent, deep
> sorrow is the breakthrough, Kierkegaard praises it:

Happy is the one in which there is true sorrow over his sins, so that the extreme unimportance to him of everything else is only the negative expression of the confirmation that one thing is unconditionally important to him . . . [This is a sickness unto life] because the life is in this, one thing is unconditionally important to him: to find forgiveness (KW 15;152).

The bronze bust of Kierkegaard which Ron commissioned for his parish shows the bespectacled philosopher in a high, broad-brimmed hat gazing ahead. The inscription reads, "I will seek my refuge with ... the Crucified One . . . to save me from myself." That humble acceptance of God's will reminds me of Ron's anniversary sermons. It also reminds me of St. Paul's admonition in Philippians, which had such impact on both Kierkegaard and his Seattle disciple, "Work out your own salvation with fear and trembling."

Ron's death in 2021 came as a great shock. He was a man of vitality and presence. He had never complained of his health. His concern was always for others. I not only felt bereft of a friend; I felt a general sorrow that the world had lost a person whose special gift was to help save us from ourselves.

Kierkegaard wanted no memorials. He requested his gravestone inscription only to read, "The Individual." Posterity wisely decided otherwise. Copenhagen is full of memorial plaques, portraits, and historical sites, and his large tombstone bears lines from a Danish poem he loved. It heartens us to remember the best who have lived among us.

Ron agreed with Kierkegaard. He wanted no praise or special attention, especially in death. His internet address said it all—*deogloria*—or better yet the version another Lutheran, J.S. Bach, used to sign all of his compositions, *Soli Deo Gloria,* "For the glory of God alone." To live and die in Christ sufficed. But like those irreverent Danes, I have to respectfully disrespect his intentions. I offer this book, inspired by his love of Kierkegaard and poetry, as a small memorial to him. There is no other poetry anthology like it, just as there is no one else quite like him. He was, like Kierkegaard, an "Individual" in the best sense of the word. May these poems remind us to rejoice that he lived among us.

HOMAGE TO SØREN KIERKEGAARD

By Dana Gioia

Work out your own salvation with fear and trembling.
—St. Paul

I was already an old man when I was born.
Small with a curved back, he dragged his leg when walking
the streets of Copenhagen. "Little Kierkegaard,"
they called him. Some meant it kindly. *The more one suffers
the more one acquires a sense of the comic.*
His hair rose in waves six inches above his head.
Save me, O God, from ever becoming sure.
What good is faith if it is not irrational?

Christianity requires a conviction of sin.
As a boy tending sheep on the frozen heath,
his starving father cursed God for his cruelty.
His fortunes changed. He grew rich and married well.
His father knew these blessings were God's punishment.
All would be stripped away. His beautiful wife died,
then five of his children. Crippled Søren survived.
The self-consuming sickness unto death is despair.

What the age needs is not a genius but a martyr.
Søren fell in love, proposed, then broke the engagement.
No one, he thought, could bear his presence daily.
My sorrow is my castle. His books were read
but ridiculed. Cartoons mocked his deformities
His private journals fill seven thousand pages.
You could read them all, he claimed, and still not know him.
He who explains this riddle explains my life.

When everyone is Christian, Christianity
does not exist. The crowd is untruth. Remember
we stand alone before God in fear and trembling.
At forty-two he collapsed on his daily walk.
Dying he seemed radiant. His skin had become
almost transparent. He refused communion
from the established church. His grave has no headstone.
Now with God's help I shall at last become myself.

INTRODUCTION

"It is a risk to preach, for as I go up into that holy place
. . . I have one listener more than can be seen, an invisible
listener . . . He looks to see whether my life expresses what
I am saying."

—*Kierkegaard's Writings* XX:234 (1850),
Practice in Christianity

In the beginning we whimper when passed over.
Later we quieted down loving the solitude, with
privacy lifting us, and aloneness pleasing us.
At the snap of a twig the deer bounds away.
Doting on us threatens where before it was just silence.
Now it doesn't hurt but is more a protection.
And so the preacher climbs the pulpit with palms
wringing wet – wishing he could talk in the dark.
But the crowd stares – and a bigger twig snaps near us.

"That Invisible Listener"
by Reverend Ronald Marshall

Ron Marshall was a brilliant scholar specializing in Kierkegaard and Luther, and his extended essays were widely published in theological and academic journals, including the *International Kierkegaard Commentary*. He also published two books, *Kierkegaard for the Church* (2013), and *Kierkegaard in the Pulpit* (2016), as well as his posthumous *Pandemic Sermons: with Continual Reference to Martin Luther* (2021). Ron served as a Lutheran parish pastor from 1979 until his early death from a brief but terminal illness in 2021. I have shared an identity with him for over fifty years as his partner and wife, and am blessed to be the mother of his three miraculous children.

Ron was a bibliophile, and upon his death his vast library provided 4500 books on theology and religion to Mekane Yesus Seminary in Addis Ababa, which represents about one-third of his wide-ranging collection. His favorite novel, and also his model, was Melville's *Moby Dick.* "In the whale . . . we see the rare virtue of a strong individual vitality, and the rare virtue of thick walls, and the rare virtue of interior spaciousness. Oh, man! Admire and model thyself after the whale! Do thou, too, remain warm among ice. Do thou, too, live in this world without being of it."[1] This was Ron.

Ron's "interior spaciousness" also included a passion for poetry. Among his vast files, I found a draft for a book of poetry based on prompts from Kierkegaard with the working title of *Improvisations on Kierkegaard*. There were over 160 prompts with their sources in *Kierkegaard's Writings* (26 volumes) translated and edited by Howard and Edna Hong, as well as Ron's creative titles based on the prompts. A few of his poems are included in this Introduction. He had also commissioned a poem for the Kierkegaard 200th Anniversary in 2013 from California Poet Laureate, Dana Gioia. Dana's stunning poem was the occasion for the friendship of the two men. In the explosion of grief following Ron's death, I sent Dana the book draft that I had stumbled upon, and he convinced me that it absolutely needed to be finished. Over 400 poems were generated in a national poetry competition through *Dappled Things* and Wiseblood Books using Ron's Kierkegaard prompts, the poets all participating in their own way with Ron's vision for a book of poetry inspired by Kierkegaard.

* * *

"It must always be kept in mind that reflection itself is not something pernicious, that on the contrary the prerequisite for acting more intensively is the thorough kneading of reflection . . . The highest and most intensive enthusiasm . . . flows on the heels of prudence and therefore perceives what is the most prudent thing to do but rejects it and thereby gains the intensity of infinite enthusiasm."

—*Kierkegaard's Writings*, KW XIV:111 (1846)
Two Ages: The Present Age and the Age of Revolution

The board is barely dusted.
Patting and molding follow.
Then the pushing down – back and forth.
Some flour's in the air.
Clumps get folded in for rising.
Beautiful arcs take shape.
My elbows and wrists start aching.
I'm thinking too soon of the oven
and how it will taste.

"Thorough Kneading of Reflection"
In Memoriam Edna H. Hong (1913-2007)
by Reverend Ronald Marshall

Would Ron be pleased with the mighty effort to complete this project? I think he would see that each poem has a life of its own, apart from his own vision. Some are more specifically tied to his prompts from Kierkegaard than others. Three of the poets (Baker, Carlson, and Di Stefano) wrote on Ron's prompt, "Blessed Restlessness," from *Upbuilding Discourses,*[2] a restlessness that Ron shared. He also identified with Kierkegaard's self-description as "Nothing But a Street-Corner Loafer" from *The Point of View,*[3] which was taken up by two of the poets (Salyer and Sullivan). Ron deeply believed that Kierkegaard was Luther's best student. And indeed "Lightning Usually Strikes Churches"[4] from *Practice in Christianity*, referenced by two of the poets (Butler and MacDonald), was taken directly from Luther's "Sermon on St. Stephen's Day," commemorating the stoning of St. Stephen.

Kierkegaard's broken engagement with his beloved Regine, thinly veiled in *Either/Or: The Seducer's Diary,*[5] was also a spark for three of the poets, (Ekstrom, O'Neill, and Houssaye). At least six of the poets (Friesen, Fullman, Grogan, Horne, Sullivan, and Schmid) wrote on the terrifying test of Abraham as the first "knight of faith" in the near-sacrifice of Isaac,[6] the subject of Kierkegaard's *Fear and Trembling,* his most widely read book. Kierkegaard's writing was, by all accounts, bewildering to most readers. Ron would be immensely pleased by the process of trying, collectively, to understand Kierkegaard and thus honor him through poetry.

* * *

"What is the comfort of the Redemption but this, that the substitute, atoning, puts himself completely in your place and in mine!"

—*Kierkegaard's Writings*, KW XVIII:123 (1849), Without Authority

Isaiah sings from all eternity
about a bad smell in the air
that chokes us. For all the bad
everywhere the good one is punished.
And our hands can't stop the nails.
Bludgeoning himself is all he can
do to help us – confounding though it be.
The deathly smell hangs around. This
is eternity's one way to help. Not any other.

"In My Place"
by Reverend Ronald Marshall

Perhaps what resonated most for Ron was Kierkegaard's dialectic between his religious despair and his deep faith in an infinitely loving God. "I will seek my refuge with the Crucified One . . . to save me from myself,"[7] from *Christian Discourses,* was framed in Ron's study. But it was his overwhelming sense that God was "Moved by all, yet Changed by Nothing," from Kierkegaard's prayer in *The Changelessness of God* (also the inspiration for poet Stadtlander), that was at the core of Ron's faith. "Even what we human beings call a trifle and unmoved pass by, the sparrow's need, that moves you; what we so often scarcely pay attention to, a human sigh, that moves you, Infinite Love. But nothing changes you, you Changeless One!"[8] He was not afraid to die because of that Infinite Love.

Ron also had an infectious laugh, especially for cartoons about logic and language which he collected in an unpublished book called *Wittgenstein and the Comics.* He was and is a Rascal-Saint (my descriptor), a "dead sinner revised and edited"[9] by Christ.

A heartfelt thank you on Ron's behalf to all who contributed to this brilliant anthology.

—Jane Harty, wife of Reverend Ron Marshall

Competition

Prize Winners

THE WRECK OF THE KØBENHAVN

By Hugh Savage, 1st Place

lost at sea with all hands, 1929

We have abandoned ship. It is snowing and a gale
blows. Tonight, while everyone is sleeping, I realize
our awful fate. Everything convinces me that this
sea has taken us beyond the limits of the world.
—message found in a bottle, washed up on the shore of
Bouvet Island, 1,600 miles east of Cape Horn, 1934.

Her figurehead the war-helmed Absalon
(Axel), founder of the town whose name she bore—
bishop of Roskilde, warrior archbishop of Lund—
fate unguessed, the five-masted barque set sail,
whose only hope—whose help in the name of the Lord—
hung not by a rope or a cord, but by the hair.

∫

From the evidence, we know the Cape was never rounded,
but where she lost her bearings have no clue;
for in the lonely wastes in which she foundered,
none but the gulls could possibly have told
—her wreck was never found—who if they knew,
give witness to the whiteness only and the cold.

From the evidence, we surmise the master blundered,
in a squall had failed to haul her wind, although,
on lookout, what masthead boy in a hundred,
(there were forty-five in training on the ship),
through snow could see—or hail the deck—the ice-floe
that like a continent was moving in?

But the evidence—the only we're possessed of,
found in a bottle a thousand miles away—
as far to the east as the Cape itself is west of
Denmark's coast and five long years gone by
(if only they had lived to sail another day!),
is the diary of a boy about to die.

ʃ

"All hands on deck! Brail up the topcourse, furl
it in the bunt. Belay, boys! Frap it fast!"
That deck, with each successive wave aswirl,
for those of the crew aloft posed death in a trice—
awash in a slosh of snow, each listing mast,
its yards encased in a treacherous glaze of ice.

"All hands!" The command was lost in the gale's roaring.
All hands together could never save the ship,
the South Atlantic through unbattened hatches pouring.
"Don't think you will see again your native town,"
they heard the tempest scream as the canvas ripped,
"or ever be warm again before you drown."

"Abandon ship!" Was she grounded, hulled, dismasted?
"Pull!" and the death-bound lifeboats pulled away.
It was snowing, we know, and the cold wind blasted,
while every boy Jack of them strove with his might and mate,
and the Humboldt Current bore them through the spray,
till the Roaring Forties drove them to their fate.

∫

Absalon: Absalom (son of David): *Ab Shalom!*
"Father of Peace", Hammer of the Wends,
conduct these sailors safely to their home—
to where the seas are not high nor the winds cold,
to where their life begins right where it ends:
a place beyond the limits of the world.

THAT WHICH CANNOT
REST CONTENT

By Paul J. Pastor, 2nd Place

Suppose there was a king who loved a humble maiden.
—Søren Kierkegaard, *Philosophical Fragments*

And in the king's good chest, suppose an anxious thought,
which counsel or rebuke could not dispel; suppose
the nibbled notion that his favor once conferred
would sour, like stale wine on last night's table;
that sudden transport up the social mountain
(the bride bathed quick in milk, dried hurriedly with sables)
might taint the downy thing that had turned magnet pole,
pulling heart's red needle; suppose the torment of the
    helpless throne,
loosing headsmen in gaunt, teary rage, dividing vertebrae
of any fool suggesting tilted unions do not herald joy; and
suppose this all stood fable for your own well-threshed
    sorrows:
now bowing under barley-weight of over-fruitful life,
now rousing the nude grief that sleeps, delicate, in love.

LIGHTNING STRIKES CHURCHES

By Jesse Keith Butler, 3rd Place

A church is a makeshifted shelter, a lean-to
thrown up against heaven, a wobbly but warm
enclosure that all the unready rush into
before the sharp edge of the storm.
When lightning strikes churches,
the pigeons know why.
They burst from their perches
and soar in the churchyard's blank sky.

A church is a fistful of feelings—it's steeple
a finger unflinchingly jabbing at clouds—
enclosing the longing the righteous can keep all
their rightness, unreached by the crowds.
When lightning strikes churches
it feels out our worth,
then, finding no purchase,
it dissipates into the earth.

A church is a monument, far out of fashion,
that clings to the crumbling brink of the land,
a ritual built between Isaac's cold question
and Abraham's trembling hand.
When lightning strikes churches
it surges with light
and restlessly searches
for faith formed unbent in the night.

A church is a boat with a broad bow to carry
the last lines of life through the world-wasting flood,
a gunnel-thin wall between us and the fury
that's frothing and foaming our blood.
When lightning strikes churches
it shudders our core.
The ship leaps and lurches
then leans to the unsighted shore.

STEALING FIGS WHILE ON HOLIDAY IN GREECE

By Nadine Ellsworth-Moran, 3rd Place

Of all the brilliant sins, affected virtues are the worst.
—Søren Kierkegaard

I can't comprehend this sky, so brilliant
on this isle, so clever, I find, blindly affected,
overwhelmed, to almost overlook my sins
hanging low, beyond a fence, sins
protected from my hands, how brilliantly
they tempt without the slightest affect
of knowledge that I am affected
by the thick scents and soft sins
their skins provoke, so brilliant
is their scheme, I must brilliant
be to release them from affliction, unaffected
as they are by sweet flesh of sins—
brilliant juice runs down my chin as I savor affection for
 my sins.

TWO-STEP

By Fr. Stephen A. Gregg, 3rd Place

This is another step, not astray
but syncopated, please, – it never lands
in old time. Write that down: The way
I play forever, improvise off-hand
the eternal pattern – step, and stop, and stand.
The incremental, everlasting race
that glorifies the simple stride, garlands
with stunned hope my failing pace,
and leaves no time to stop, untethers grace.
Help me. Now. I cannot win.
I maybe, only barely, recall your face,
and this I think is what they mean by "sin."
To love and to be loved is all my care.
I make another step. Please meet me there.

"FROM THE PAPERS OF ONE STILL LIVING"

By Matthew Carey Salyer, 3rd Place

Søren pseudonymous, haunted by lambs.
Hans Christian Anderson love-shy in his golden age.
Europe as iambs of revolution at barricades.
The two men so at such a time a tale of two
transformations. Faith a tallow candle.
Once I was young, polemical, and I wore out
the idea of history like a boot's old sole.
Now I would never try to cobble its riddle.
At Penn Station, night eats me. Memory stirs me.
I was a streetcorner loafer, an idler, Søren said,
a frivolous bird. He saw likewise a wit without
earnestness in Anderson's fairy tales, the acrid,
ironic heartsickness of Thumbelina's swallow
or the steadfast tin soldier, his ballerina's burned
spangle. If I fear, I fear I'm the last Times Square outcast
in the yarn of New York, a talking, disentangled rat
that thinks (as a man might) a name might
be some magical talisman working against harm.

I view everything aeterno modo, Søren writes.
So suppose I were a Kierkegaard, meaning church farm.
Then I'd die in something that belonged to my father.
Suppose that I'd died a child. He might've carried me,
dug his shallow furrow in an ø, and planted me there,
whispering something overhead that only I could hear.
Ø suppose my father were alive to hear me now.
In midtown, melting into the legs of a leaden crowd,
I am constantly aeterno modo. For God's sake,
look at the hideousness of the swans in Central Park
or the beautiful childishness of tourists craning
their necks to see rooflines scrub the white doll
skin of heaven, skein of a thought with my name.

POEMS

SETTLED

By Christina Baker

*. . . a believer cannot sit still as one sits with a pilgrim's
staff in one's hand—a believer travels forward.*
                              —Søren Kierkegaard

My family lived in the same house
the entirety of my childhood.
My daughter, on the other hand,
remembers six of her seven homes.

Seventh time's the charm,
with mortgage, braces, minivan—
It is a temptation to cling
to this house, this job, this life.

I think of the Benedictines.
today's mail—a fruitcake
and fudge catalog—reminds me
of their vow of stability.

Who could be more settled than that?
Yet they are never still—
always praying, working,
pressing cheeses. Pressing hearts

towards God—Is that so different
from laundry, dishes, bedtime
stories? Prayer before meals,
chaplet in the carpool line?

Despite all the motion, I'm restless.
Despite seeming settled,
we keep moving forward—
crawling to walking,

listening to speaking to listening,
roots delving for the depths,
branches stretching for the heights—
never, and always, the end in sight.

THE KIERKEGAARDIAN
OATH OF AUTHENTICITY

by Paul Bussan

I do solemnly swear,
upon pain of blasphemy,
me, the whole me,
and nothing but me,
so help me, God, to be.

BLESSED RESTLESSNESS

By Lauren K. Carlson

*What I am seeking is not here, and for that very
reason I believe it.*

—Søren Kierkegaard

Were the arrow pulled out
though you're not supposed to

tear an opening in the veil.
The dark line of your fascia

a boiled red rope, the skin a curtain.
A red current, the cup inside you tipped.

You're supposed to be filled
with its—the arrow's—potions. Faith.

Instead, you've torn into an emptiness,
the ribcage around the heart's chambers

like potter's hands, caressing both
what is and isn't yet—

After the arrow hits the heart
after the potter throws the clay

you're supposed to wait,
you're supposed to be shaped.

But what's vessel without emptiness,
potential without material.

The cupful absent thirst,
form without ash.

BLESSED RESTLESSNESS

By Dante Di Stefano

The future I'm trying to recollect
keeps digging into me like windshield glass
in my pocket digging into my thigh
as I hang upside down in a totaled

Honda on a country road that curves like
an ampersand or the communion cup
I lifted to my lips so many Sundays
ago when all of life unfolded in

the hushed queendom of Ordinary Time—
like the serenity ached in my knuckles
as I prayed the rosary was really

a kind of flight I was spinning toward—
like I was inside a skipping stone &
no vast darknesses bookended my life.

KIERKEGAARD'S PROPOSAL

By Max Roland Ekstrom

Outside the piano studio you listen
as Regine and her future husband
trade bars of Haydn, her hands
guiding the grand piano like a barge
through narrows, and you wish
you could blind yourself to its sight.
You will propose first, presenting her
this sapphire, smoothing over your tie
and the loan your father once stood you
that in death he has at last forgiven.
As they advance the measure into a sea
of dappling joy, you imagine her ripening
smile as the September sun stoops
over the city block whose windows
you witness as slabs of granite.
Your eyes climb the mountain
of your proposal—Regine bearing
your son and cooking your Sunday
roast that you can almost smell—
the fat grays on the surface,
the wood within the stove cracks
while the cheap wine cuts like a knife.

DYSMONIUM

By Michial Farmer

The drunkard's choir of my psyche, divided
Not into four parts, but into half a million,
Howls its alley-cat songs night and day, forever
Racing ahead and lagging behind the hapless
Conductor's wagging baton. "Purity of heart,"
Said Kierkegaard, "is to will one thing," to transform
The lunatic cacophony into plainchant—
A ruler's single line, the mathematical
Precision of the passionless, musical spheres.

BURNT OFFERING

By LaDonna Friesen

Based on the scene of Abraham and Isaac in Genesis 22

I have held knives in fires,
The unburned burning blade,
Readied for cutting breath—
The goat, the ram, the lamb—

Now

When my nearly-singed hand lifts the blade,
I see my son's eyes tendered in the metal.
He is lying just there at the turn of my shoulder,
his body fragrant with wood, eyes open to the sky,
his soft olive arms splayed on stone.

"Father," he says,
I kneel, the knife searing up like a pillar of fire
"The lamb?"
The light shifts on the blade, the moon rises
as the sun sets, my heart lurches

as a tongue of fire whispers on the soft flesh
at the back of my knee.
"God offers his own lamb, my son."

Father, I murmur, do you move,
Are you moved?
Rubbing my thumb over the blade,
I nick the soft flesh of my thumb
as silence burns into the sound of my name
and a ram's horn startles leaves in the thicket,
orange-singed in the last flame of day.

A ram cries but not my son
and I am on my knees, arms crossed
over Isaac's heart. His chest rises, his breath rushes.
Ash, scabbed in the crevices of my soul, falls away
and smarts new skin, new knowing.
Father, moved but unmoving,
You do not change.
I lift my son to my chest
like a blossoming branch, rising from ash.

JOHANNES DE SILENTIO SPEAKS

By Joshua S. Fullman

But, no—I can't. I, mere sophist, lack grace
and understanding, not knowing how I'd act
hearing my child's cry. Without figures, facts,
or logic, language fails, and I can't face

what wild convulsions scream within my chest.
For, forced to choose between absurdity
and bleak annihilation, how can I see—
and which is which?—between the darknesses

and babble? How could I root up the tree
joining me to all humanity, will
my own will's death, cloak myself in evil—
all to satiate phantom vagaries,

a hunger more demonic than divine?
All I see are the unknowable wells
of consciousness: and there, above the hells
of unreason, stands a grim knight consigned

to the abyss, a prisoner cast out
to an icy night. Falling from the light,
he plunges, shadow within shadow, like
a stone beneath the fatal deeps of doubt

and black despair. And just when his lungs break
with fear and swallow death, he rises tall,
assured he'll walk the obsidian pall
of waves below. How can I follow, take

the place of him I scorn? How damn my life
by faith? How curse myself with good?
                         Then through
a glass of words, I catch the changing hue
and see the grieving father raise his knife.

GIMÉNEZ ADDRESSES
THE VIRGIN OF MERCY

By Daniel Galef

This is the result of two hours of devotion to the Virgin of Mercy.
—the painter of the fresco portrait of Christ in Borja, Spain

We've both produced a Christ—Yours was of flesh
and mine of mural plaster. Both predate
our pure conception. Frescos must be fresh,
but light, and life, are old. All art came late.
The fallacy of Zeuxis and Parrhasius
was thinking that the Lord demands good taste.
As long as we are modest, kind, and chaste,
then Heaven takes our prayers, a Dios gracias.
Who cares just how in-tune a psalm is sung,
how clear the voice, or if it keeps good time?
The spirit's in the heart, and not the tongue.
All art is re-Creation. On wet lime
like on the skin of water we can limn
and—if we mean it—it will be a hymn.

REREADING *FEAR AND TREMBLING*

By Mia Schilling Grogan

God equals mother. Abraham is breast.
Isaac the infant to be weaned.
The one who can't look away, obsessed

with re-imagining the story, twinned
it by analogy with breastfeeding,
offering scenarios Silencio gleaned

from hearsay, one presumes, or by reading
maxims – the blackened tit a strategy
that sounds real, but is it? After conceding

in the "Exordium" that human sympathy
fails as exegesis, we're off through art
and beyond ethics to valorize not tragedy's

hero, but the knight of faith.
                                    I sat apart
in my seminar on Kierkegaard and Nietzsche,
years ago, off to the side, doodling a heart

in the margin of my notebook, writing preachy
letters to friends, enraged by the futile
roaming of philosophy in times of need – edgy

rebellion for a straight-A student. For the final,
I spent a weekend cramming and regretting.
I should have questioned or debated this brutal

reading: Abraham cannot speak without negating
paradox or ceasing to be self? Silence, then, before
Sarah who would have stopped him?

                                                    Letting-

down is reflexive, something I learned years later
and years ago, now. Now, when I reread this
book, mostly I worry about Søren – all his fear-

filled titles, clear evidence of anxiety, of a sickness
we treat today. Honestly, I wish for him a life
with Regine and the freedom for the greatness

he achieved, not either/or. And I imagine Love,
or Governance, in that moment of his death,
bending over him, the phantom reflex of

release warming her breast, crooning with
Søren this psalm, Surely, I have behaved
myself, like one weaned . . . , easing his breath-

less entrance into abundance.

THE SAME SHARED RISK, THE SAME SHARED SALVATION

By Jefferson Holdridge

1

When Aeneas escaped Troy as it was sacked
And stopped to take his young son by the hand,
While carrying his ancient father on his back,
He answered more than simply an Oedipal riddle.
Salvation demands more than legs to stand
For Isaac and Emmanuel — for civilization
Reborn beyond survival and Roman piety.
For greater sacrifice, like those who travel
A thousand miles or more, leaving family
Afraid, risking contagion, to shoulder the sick
(And reflect at night on what they've seen and done),
Whose recovery or descent remains unknown.
They come to comfort a lonely, feverish city
And patients who without them die alone.

11

Scoured now, its scaffolding stowed,
The Rialto Bridge is bone white
As before La Salute's dome had glowed.

The parting ebb-tide has fully risen.
The sun that had set is at full height.
The nearest bridge once draped in plastic

Today permits our homesick sight.
Even to the same, the return is drastic.
It means we must recast this light

As Titian had depicting sin
In the Sacristy: Cain and Abel,
Isaac bound and the decollation

Of Goliath in a triptych fable
In which blind faith and heroism
Answer the anger of a jealous killing.

The founding blow is struck again
Though changed in Tintoretto's prism
Through miracle if God is willing.

The Wedding of Cana, water to wine.
The table dividing women from men
As Christ in a nimbus makes a sign.

THREE PORTRAITS OF ABRAHAM

By E. Edward Horne

He knew there was no use crying out, for none of them would save him.

—Czesław Miłosz, *Study of Loneliness*

Prelude (at a goat roast in the Shenandoah Valley)

To look a creature in her oblong eyes
and thank her for her life and draw the blade
across her neck with pressure, to cut cleanly
the artery so the lifeblood pours and puddles
in the grass, it takes something like courage,
but it isn't courage. Bound and bleeding
between two worlds, a being both yet neither:
she is a goat with goaty aspirations,
nothing but caprice and care for kids,
and she is our dinner.

I. Portrait of Abraham the night before

But how will it come to pass? He cannot see beyond
the wood, the knife, the fire. Perhaps the blood
will uncongeal, draining back into Isaac's heaped body
until a violent shudder opens the eyes with their look
of pained betrayal. Or, he will sweep the blade again
back across the man's thick neck, healing the wound
between father and son. This is tomorrow's worry—
Still, his hands shake. The lunate horn glows
with embers by his side. Night creatures keep distant.
They know to avoid a disturbed and resolute heart.

II. Portrait of Abraham in the act

After putting his hand to the plow on Mt. Moriah,
does Abraham look back over the hills, farsighted,
seeing into Sarah's tent as she collapses and clasps
at her breast, breathless and bereft? Does he foresee
the silent three days back and what he will say, seeing
in her eyes their son? Raised arm and knife in hand,
does his chest split like firewood, a flaming brazier
passing through the halves of his heart?
He is not cutting a covenant he is cutting off everything
and everyone. For Abraham, there will be no going back.

III. Portrait of father and son, after the sacrifice

In the grass in the valley with the goat, my son
is three years old and watches as I skin the hide.
Clumsily I wield the knife while he stares,
baptized in realization of death and blood.
Later he will wake from dreams to tell my wife
he doesn't want daddy to kill him with a knife.
Forgive me father, for I have only sinned.
I haven't faith enough to go beyond, with burning heart
to bind my son. I admire Abraham for his honest murder,
but father, I keep from you my best.

THE PASSIONS OF SØREN KIERKEGAARD

By Ron Houssaye

Young Søren was called The Fork because he would
  discern a person's flaw
then stick them with it, not cruelly, but just to humor
  himself.
Inside he battled despair and on his body he suffered a
  spinal deformity.
Yet, somehow he pushed forward beyond childhood pain,
  except a spiritual
scar remained, inherited from his father, a thorn from his
  youthful trials.
Even this he turned to profit, as a challenge to accept and
  overcome.

Although love slipped his grasp it was not for lack of his
     lover's devotion.
Regine Olsen gave herself to him, only to have him
     unselfishly leave her.
He felt she should not have to suffer a certain oddness
     about his personality.
In time Copenhagen was too small for his ambitions to
     write and publish.
So to Berlin he traveled, in 1841, like a squire hoping to
     become a knight.
He would join philosophy to theology with his own
     clever, unorthodox style.

In Berlin he felt at home for the first time, but his inner
     battles continued.
Psychiatry could not come to his aid; so he relied on
     faith and determination.
A dark pit of mental agony often came, with cycles of
     despair and exhilaration.
Though he could not give birth to a child, he gave birth
          to *Either/Or,*
a "double edged little dagger," he wrote, adding ironically,
"I have one more intimate confidant – my melancholy."

The most delightful passion of Søren Kierkegaard may
   well be *Irony*.
To confirm this we may consider his dissertation,
   The Concept of Irony.
In *The Apology*, Socrates explains why the Oracle called
   him the wisest man in Athens.
He was the wisest because he was aware of his ignorance,
   while others were not.
Søren viewed Socrates steeped in irony during his trial
before the Athenian Court.
Therefore, *tragic* is not a word that fits S.K., nor can it be
part of his legacy.

CRUCIFY HIM

By Tristan Macdonald

[H]ow strange that [lightning] does not strike ev-
ery Sunday in order to hit that type of preaching,
which is nothing but a kind of dissoluteness, for the
speaker falsely ascribes to himself and his listeners
something that is not at all true of them.
                                    —Søren Kierkegaard

In the Passion narrative at the Palm Sunday Mass,
the priest broke from the prescribed liturgy,
assigning us Your part instead of the crowd's,
hoping to spare our mouths of the distasteful,
murderous words of "crucify him, crucify him."

So I sat and stewed, pissed at the priest's decision
to distance us from sinners—a Pharisaical decision—
and I spoke the crowd's words loudly and proudly,
wanting to rise and rebel in the American way:
a lone cowboy against an errant sheriff.

But I found myself distracted at the holiest moment,
one eye on Your sacrifice but both eyes on myself,
almost blinded to You by my heightened sense of I;
when I grabbed the chalice into which I'd made You bleed,
I couldn't feel blood's heat, but the golden chill of Pharisees.

KIERKEGAARD AT GILBJERG

By Dan MacIsaac

No sail turned like a page on the chronicle
of the sea. The view was a harmony
of horizon, of ocean and heaven
unbroken by spar or jutting mast.

The philosopher stood on the high shore
before dead calm, rapt past logic, beyond words.
Beneath him lay stones once raked by glacial ice
and from the thickets hailed vespers of wrens.

And he was carried into the embrace
of his elders until gulls screeching
like the ungreased wheels of a hay cart
shattered his reverie and he was cast out.

The seer wallowed in a dark slough of thought,
blinded and pummeled by bleak dialectics
until he was meekly restored by light
like candleglow on an emptied tomb.

EXPECTING

By Mara Matteoli

Then come the prayers no longer blessed with scents
Of expectation, but the faintest whiff
Of understanding: no count of double lines,
Of beating hearts that someday tune themselves
To hers can slow the thumping of her soul.

Perhaps it's just as well; perhaps to ease
Some hungers here would leave some taste of Eve's
Travails unsavored. But left with a womb
Unstretched, unburdened, she can bless the pangs
Of gnawing for the things that are not here.

And all is blessing, for if her hands were full
Too soon, she might forget the emptiness
That all must carry, gestating for nine
Decades, less or more, until the birth
Of death can show us what it was we sought.

She thinks of souls like bottles all lined up;
Some small, some large, all waiting to receive
The mother's milk that quenches every thirst -
But even small souls must have empty space
That Love can fill, or else be poured all out.

FOR LOVE, I DREAM-WALK

By Danielle McMahon

stumble dumb into deep mists
of pining, valleys of ponderous aster
& lily, poppy & violet, carried in wisps

of cold light, I dream-walk
to the river's starless mouth,

to the jagged edge of memory,
beguiled by strange music.

The Unreal calls me here to the edge,
compels me to bend low,

kiss the cool lips of my love-
bygone, my stinging poppy-blossom, my
dream-song, she

wades here in the deepest
black waters & cries out:

I am the arrow and the pull
I am the mouth of the drowned girl

I am the snaking path of cobble
I am of root, of sinew & knot

I am the ravenous, the leaden
I fix my gaze to keep

I yowl in the name of my love
I bathe in pools of sepia-tone

I, a silken tongue
upon jagged rock,

will not be silent

ISSUES OF BLOOD

By Sharon Fish Mooney

. . . she told no one else what she had in mind and
what she believed—she said very softly to herself, "If I
only touch the hem of his robe I shall be healed." The
secret she kept to herself; it was the secret of faith
which saved her both for time and eternity.
                    —Søren Kierkegaard, *Works of Love*

For twelve long years I suffered and spent all
I'd saved from selling bread to try and rid
my body from the dread disease that bled
me dry. Physicians all, they worthless were
who poked and pried and told me that they knew
a cure but needed more from me. More coins!
My livelihood was lost and I was left
with but the strength of will to beg my bread
from others who were better off than I.

But then I saw him standing there, the one
I'd heard had healed the lame, the blind, the deaf
and knew he was the answer to my prayer
that day. But who was I? A woman clothed
in sin and shame, unclean, unworthy to
call out his name. I stumbled, and then stretched
my hand to touch his robe and felt the fount
within me dry and suddenly I knew
I had been healed by a physician kind.

The crowd pressed in on him and yet he asked
them who had been the one to touch him so
that power had flowed forth like blood out from
his side to heal this one who had in tears
with fear and trembling at his feet fell down.
"My daughter, know your faith has made you whole
this day so go in peace and be set free
from all thy scourge. Take courage for your faith
has been your hope, your cure—your faith in Me."

TESTAMENT

By Sean O'Neill

What God, if not a master and a Lord?
Yet lover too, the friend who breaks the dark
and plunges at the heart, not with the sword,
but with the punctured palm, to leave his mark
upon the bloodied soul and fan that spark
that blows to greatness with the watered brow.
His mercy spills what pilgrim hearts avow.

I trudge these grimy streets of narrow bends,
the crooked alleys where the beggars dwell,
and press their hands with alms to make amends
for all the evils they have supped from hell.
Philosophy has never savored this quaint smell
that gathers in the gutters where they squat,
nor winkled sense from what cannot be taught.

My love I sacrificed to find the key,
the purpose and the aim of living here,
some truth that's truthful, true enough for me,
some word or love to which I can adhere,
subjective though it may at first appear.
To know myself and strip the immortal soul
reveals each naked segment of the whole.

My journals prove the fire of love misspent
when I was affianced to dear Regine.
Yet I am of a melancholic bent
and am no suitor fit for such a queen.
For heaven knows the sickness I have seen,
the sickness unto death that made me quit
that love, myself a beggar, I admit.

The will of God emerges from the mist,
then disappears as though a heavy cloud
of doubt descended like a falling fist,
while every night my conscience cries aloud,
"Will no one save me from this winding shroud
that billows from the grave within my mind?"
Yet onward to the finish, stern but blind.

My fragments mutter in the dark and fall
away and all my written testament
has come to naught; yes, every scrawl
I penned to prove the Crucified has bent
His love toward us. That love is never spent
but comes at sudden times to still and calm
the troubled heart and steep the soul in balm.

Now, at the end, my dying wish is this:
to see not what is wrong and what is right,
but simply to believe that in one kiss
of love from God the density of night
is lessened as I fall into His light.
The dark is drawing near for everyone,
yet I will turn to Love as to the sun.

FOR MY CHILDREN

By Michael J. Ortiz

For each of you I would plant a garden,
dig earth, clay the color of faded blood,

mix my sweat with sunlight and rock,
cart in manure, topsoil, sturdy bordering

stones fashioned on precisely measured
lines drawn in earth's rich ecliptic.

I would worry over my soil's acidity, lie
awake at night calculating its relative elements

of lime and composted bitters from my
fields and grasses, work each of the stones

to wedge them just right, cornicing all
the odorous legends of peat-born story:

Rosemary for soothing oils, lilies to
evoke eternity, Nightshade for intruders,

wild violets, English bluebells for shattered
calm, Rue to cleanse the heart, hyssop

to fend off cloying ease, Spring Snowflake
for poise, quinces for memory, and more:

the jagged holly for winter's icy vigils,
the tart bewitching taste of mandrake that

only lovers share, rough-hewn huts of
oak for nurseries, where shoots and cuttings

may break free in the austere days of early
spring, harbingers of heady summer.

To all this have my hands inured, hard
as a mattock's handle, my nails half-moons

of dirt, soil clinging to the crossroads
of my laboring and untiring freedoms.

Even in December, when the holly hones its
points on the burrs of winter, my gardens

will sleep mindful, retentive, their deep wells
bearing in moving skies all the tomorrows

I wish for you, full of seasons of sweat
and rest, life's enduring, intricate harvest.

PRAYER BEFORE A SERMON IN THE NAVE

By Karl Plank

Since we found that the union could not be brought about by an elevation it must be attempted by a descent.
—Søren Kierkegaard, *Philosophical Fragments*

Uphold Thou me
that I may lift up
the heavy-hinged hatch
that seals us in the hold
of captive cargo.
We fumble in the dark, hands up
to feel our way in gestures
of surrender or pleadings
to stop, to stay away.
We have touched the walls,
seen the absence of light
and now would ascend
to the trapdoor, a ladder of bodies.
Reach out, I cry, *that I may lift up*
Thee.

TEAR OUT THIS PAGE
IN THE BOOK OF LIES

By Lois Roma-Deeley

So is this what my days will look like now—
reopened, resumed, retuned, restarted,
like over-winding antique clocks, the how
requires a key. These moments, my most unguarded,
will likely kill me. Time's the brute I know
who stalks the city streets, then soon departs—
it'll bring me to my knees and, bowing down,
I'll yield. But what of it? My true remorse
unrests my soul—I dare not let it show—
the beast which skulks along beside me wants
to leap on strangers, neighbors, sweethearts, kin.
I watch all his inadvertent ways
click off the broken hours of days grown thin.
Love or fear? He spins the wheel. And I wait.

SARAH COMPLAINS TO THE LORD ABOUT KIERKEGAARD

By Joyce Schmid

What did Abraham? All the while he had faith, believing that God would not demand Isaac of him, though ready all the while to sacrifice him, should it be demanded of him . . . He was, to be sure, surprised at the outcome . . . On this height, then, stands Abraham . . . He does really proceed further, he arrives at faith.
                    —Søren Kierkegaard, *Fear and Trembling*

O Heavenly Father, Søren had it wrong!
My husband Abram was deranged.
There was a reason why he wouldn't tell me
of his cockamamie plan.
And faith? Which one of us had faith—
my Abram who thought You so bloodthirsty
you would order him to kill our only son—
the man who grabbed a knife and tied his child
to a stack of wood, prepared to cut his throat?
or me, his wife, the one who knew
the voice he thought he heard could not
have been Your Voice, the loving Voice of God?

You watched in disbelief
as Abram saddled up his ass,
took two young helpers and our Isaac
to the Mountains of Moriah for the sacrifice,
but You had faith in Abram,
You believed he would awaken from insanity.
Not until he tied poor Isaac up,
stretched forth his hand and actually
raised the knife to slay his son
did You step in and send an angel to command,
"Lay not thine hand upon the lad,"
an angel too polite to add, "You lunatic."

But even after this,
You kept Your faith
in Your imperfect Abraham
who so misunderstood You—
you multiplied his seed like stars in heaven,
or like grains of sand swept out to sea each day,
only to return again as jewels.
O God, you never would demand
we close our hearts to all you've given us.
You've designed Your people on this earth
to love Your world as You do,
holding tight to every last display of light.

SØREN, YOUR SPIRIT
STILL HAUNTS ME NOW

By G. E. Schwartz

Søren, Your spirit haunts me now: you picture
My condition as if etched on copper by Rembrandt,
    But always in the otherness of a pseudonym.
The cloud-dancing pellucidity of your prose

    Has a retroflexed gloss forbidding transparency.
When I list to that still small voice I hear your
    Laughter, the laughter of an author full out of
The tumult of genius. And I imagine from

Your emphasis on *my* self that my God is not
Other, I am arrested by his shadow in which
    The face of the beloved is as a candle snuffed
Out in the darkness following on, always on,

The mind's dazzling explosion. Either way
There is terror. Backwards there's the fells
    In Jutland, like the shores of Ontario, where
Our fathers from the Calvaries of themselves,

Stood iron accusing God. Søren, forward we
Are ones overtaken by speed, our own willful
    Speed, thoughts brought to bay by truths as
Opaque as their reflections, running to prayers,

    Clear as glass that, beginning in obscurity as
Our books do, the longer we stare into that
    Clearer becomes the reflection of a profile,—
Instilling hope to flickering wills, pointing to

    The blue beyond sky's gray, and there,—there,
    Always other than our own.

BORN AGAIN

By Richard Spilman

Now after so many tears,
so much recrimination,
when a new birth reveals
its soft crown of reason,

when the tight fist
you've clenched so long
unfurls, adds its cry
of freedom to your pain,

as the future lies
gasping in your arms,
eyes pinched against light,
demanding to be fed,

what can you say as you
nurse this new, holy,
and blood-stained genesis
but Yes, my darling, yes?

YOU, MOVED

By Alyssa Stadtlander

On the corner across from the drugstore, someone's child
is clutching a cardboard sign—yesterday,
it was a barefoot girl bold enough to wander
right into the the street and *tap tap tap*
on the thick glass borders of the cars.
Today it is a dog and an old man
holding up his handwritten plea: *Hard times.*
Anything helps. I consider

crossing the street. But you, moved
with compassion (that's what the text says)
reach towards and touch. The philosopher wrote
that everything moves you and in infinite
love, while we move across
roads, cities, countries so we don't have to look

at the sparrow falling out of the burning nest,
don't have to hear the sighs of the mothers
locking their front doors, don't catch
the stale scent of the man and his dog
on the corner, lest we too become infected
with misfortune; we are so frightened

of becoming like You. O changeless
one who lets yourself be moved, your heart turns
over heavy tables as you search for those lost
things: our hearts turning
to stone in the tidy darkness
of our tremendous lack, in our hidden longing
for your wild, messy heaven.

PNEUMA

By Jeanette W. Stickel

*What is a poet? An unhappy person who conceals
profound anguish in his heart but whose lips are so
formed that as sighs and cries pass over them they
sound like beautiful music.*
                                        —Søren Kierkegaard

He was a small man,
sitting on a stool near the altar—
his legs too bent to stand for long

but when he lifted his trumpet,
brought the mouthpiece
to his lips, his breath,

shaped by the instrument,
poured into the sanctuary,
bright and brassy,

brilliant. My thoughts lifted
with the high notes—
what sound would come forth

from his breath through
a tuba or flute? Fashioned
by the form it passes through—

same breath, vast variety,
as we, various vessels, filled with
God's sighs produce unique tones.

Pass though me Breath of Life,
make my notes pure—shape the music
of my broken life by your spirit,

make it one with yours.

GRACE

By Stuart Stromin

I fell into a sweet pit
of depravity
pulled into the pell-mell
by its own gravity.
Everything was open
to experiment and exposure
in a decadent descent
with no rigid enclosure.

The free fall filled me
with exhilaration,
stripped to my soul
on a feast of sensation,
and since I am here confessing,
I admit the taste of sin
was more like a blessing.

You would think blessings
are for the deserving
but the way that the arc
of the universe is curving,
even a wretch can be rewarded
no matter how licentious,
luscious or sordid.

I received more than my share,
carousing and caressing,
and count each joyful moment
as bounty and blessing,
emerging purified from the den
to see with full clarity,
the less in my merit
the more in the charity.

KIERKEGAARD'S TREMENDOUS PARADOXES

By Roseanne T. Sullivan

Sloucher crooked like a human question mark.
Flaneur of Copenhagen, Street-corner loafer.
Unscientific method-ist, proto-existentialist
Godseeker labeled philosopher by posterity.

Writing the opposite of what you intend.
Shifting persona. Hinting at ephemera.
Mystifying readers, teasing out truth.
How do I know you? Let me count the ways.

Humanities 101. Brandeis Freshman.
Great-genius-wannabe-me. Why study long-dead
Philosophers like Aristotle and you,
I sniffed, who got so much so wrong years ago?

Now at 77 I know you better, a recent taste
Acquired doing research to write this poem,
You who only knew post-Catholic Danish
Worship services with hours-long sermons.

Congregations dozing behind glazed eyes.
Memorized verses filed in their heads.
You weird-bodied sensitive like some of us who get you,
Heard Scripture as the living Word it is.

You eavesdropped when God told Father Abraham
To sacrifice Isaac, belov'd child of His promise.
Journeyed with that father, that son, the knife,
The binding rope, the fuel. Until with great relief . . .

You all caught sight of the ram. Then you pondered
Whether Isaac ever got over his near immolation
By his own father's hand. And why Abraham
Set his face like flint to do that monstrous deed.

Suspension of morality? Obedience über alles? I think not.
Did you forget or overlook what St. Paul told us?
Abraham walked with Him so long and knew Him so well.
He reasoned God could raise Isaac from the dead.

And why didn't you consider this either, how later,
Much later after Abraham's multitudinous offspring
Were long settled in the promised land, astoundingly
God Himself enabled what He asked Abraham to do?

OTHERNESS

By Tavner Threatt

If you gaze long into an abyss, the abyss also gazes into you.
—Nietzsche

l once read
if eye contact spreads
past five seconds
you're about to be killed
or kissed.

A near miss
spells a big difference-
joy or disaster.
The heart beats faster
when the mind doesn't know.

Which goes to show
what Kierkegaard said,
that man's life is dread,
is much worse
than an imposed curse.

Freedom, love and death,
are the ultimate tests.
Between fear's intensity
and hope's dependence on mystery,
we wait—but viscerally.

When we stare back, we finally see
beyond what we perceive.
Lost in an iris and attuned to silence,
being-toward-divine-darkness,
only the unknown can surprise us.

TWO SHIPS

By Catalina Margarita Udani

How could anyone have much time for human minutiae
when he is heading, under the full sail of hope, toward
the perfect? But if apostolic speech is always as impa-
tient as a woman in labor, then the two considerations
in particular are likely to stir up even more—on the one
hand, the idea that the night is over and day has broken,
that the night has lasted long enough and the point is to
use the day; on the other hand, the idea that the time is
coming when one can no longer work, that the days are
numbered, the end is near, that the end of all things is
approaching.

—"Impatient As a Woman in Labor,"
KW V:69 from 18 *Upbuilding Discourses*

I am sailing twice, to opposite poles, and in my two ships
    I lattice the world
both by night and by day. My ship that sees sun presses
    on to perfection
as the other chases the shade.
I know twice that there remains little time.

Here on my ships, where I face south and north,
there is glass on the air and chill on my spine
and the sails are filled with wanting.
The work has begun and is soon ended.

My child to be born on these two journeys will come to
    the cool of a thousand stars
and the mantle of the flaming sun. I will embrace him
    until he must come to shore
where the land will hate him.
He will bring wind there, to the end of the sea.

And where the sea runs out my ships will continue,
    crossing the world by the wind of his breath
glass melting into rain for their hearts to grow
to glow and to fill with wanting.
He gave me unnumbered time.

THE RUMOR OF
YOUR SWEETNESS

By Joseph Walls

How fitfully we haunt this crumbling place
called home! You're perfect, they say
just where you are. So we stay here,
drifting among our shabby furniture,
repeating our lessons: "Perfection is nothing–
nothing more than myself." We linger self-sufficient
in our dark rooms, by turns exultant and mournful.
Sometimes we stand in the yard and gaze
down the road. Our restless feet are subdued
by rows of posted signs–no thru, no traffic,
no outlet.

Shall we step into the road where wind
scatters the dead leaves, bends every stalk,
gesturing onward? Will we let the first
sweet strides sweep us away,
allow rain to wash from us the dust of the old life?
Can we forsake all the shops, bars and brothels
that flash "home" in bright letters?
Who will come and go with me?
Must I go alone to the end of all loneliness?

Holy Spirit, Beckoning Wind,
if you cannot entice me, blow down my pitiful shack.
Christ, My Way, remember my thin legs
and fickle feet. Give me to lean on
the wood of your cross, and let your cross
be the true signpost at every turning.
Father, my Home, salt my thirst and ruin my rest.
May the rumor of Your sweetness
turn the food that cannot nourish
to dust in my mouth. For it is better to be homeless
on the road to home, than haunt forever
this empty house.

SABBATH CANDLES

By Will Wells

[L]et ourselves be brought up, . . . by your changeless-
ness to find rest and to rest in your changelessness.
> —Søren Kierkegaard

As Shabbos candles shrink, flames climb higher
on ever-longer wicks, like wakes that raft
the flotsam of our acts. They rise, quiver
or sink, responsive both to breath and drafts
that circulate within the house, unseen.
First lit as evening falls, their flickering
and flares enact the human struggle between
despair and hope, that balanced bickering.

Hanukkah, Diwali, or midnight Mass
on Christmas Eve, our urge to light the dark
confesses fundamental loneliness.
And melting tallow mimes our mortal work.
Hear us, O Lord, whatever you may be,
and guide our fading to eternity.

SONNET FOR SOME OF US

By Gail White

Blessed are those who take what they can get.
Who marry someone who is not the greatest
beauty or athlete that they've ever met.
Blessed are those who do not have the latest
technology at command. Who do not speak
three languages. Who cry when something hurts.
Blessed are those whose drive to win is weak,
stock market failures, poets, introverts.
Blessed are those who choose to live alone
with dogs or cats rather than make a speech,
who never go exploring on their own
or try for anything beyond their reach.
Blessed, who know they'd fail so shun the test
and settle down, settling for second best.

SØREN KIERKEGAARD BIOGRAPHY

Søren Kierkegaard (1813–1855)[10] was born on May 5th, 1813 in Copenhagen, Denmark. He was the seventh and last child of wealthy hosier, Michael Pedersen Kierkegaard and Ane Sørensdatter Lund, a former household servant and distant cousin of Michael Kierkegaard. Ane was Michael Kierkegaard's second wife, and he married her within a year of his first wife's death and four months into Ane's first pregnancy. Michael Kierkegaard was a deeply melancholic, sternly religious man who carried a heavy burden of guilt, which he imposed on his children.

The family's surname derived from the fact they were indentured to the parish priest, who provided a piece of the church (*Kirke*) farm (*Gaard*) for the family's use. The name Kirkegaard (in older spelling Kierkegaard) more commonly means 'churchyard' or 'cemetery.' A sense of doom and death seemed to hover over Michael Kierkegaard for most of his 82 years. Although his material fortunes soon turned around dramatically, he was convinced that he had brought a curse on his family and that all his children were doomed to die by the age attained by Jesus Christ. Of Michael's seven children, only his sons Peter and Søren survived beyond this age.[11]

As a young man, Søren Kierkegaard attended the University of Copenhagen. During that time, he met a woman named Regine Olsen. They were engaged to be married, but Kierkegaard broke off the engagement with no explanation in 1841. He graduated that same year with a dissertation called *On the Concept of Irony with Continual Reference to Socrates* (1841).[12] Søren Kierkegaard began publishing books under various pseudonyms, including Johannes Climacus and Johannes de Silentio. In his later years, Kierkegaard opposed the leaders of the Lutheran Church of Denmark. He wrote about his philosophical issues with Christendom, which he deemed the merging of church and society.

Kierkegaard was an astonishingly prolific writer whose work—almost all of which was written in the 1840s—is difficult to categorize, spanning philosophy, theology, religious and devotional writing, literary criticism, psychology and social critique. Kierkegaard's mode of philosophizing owes much of its approach to the ancients, particularly his hero Socrates, though his work also draws strongly and creatively on the Bible and other Christian sources. Several major themes in his work include anxiety and despair, subjectivity, absurdism, aesthetics, ethics, and religion.

In 1855, Kierkegaard collapsed in the streets of Copenhagen. He spent a month in the hospital and died in October of that same year at the age of forty-two.

AUTHOR BIOGRAPHIES

HUGH SAVAGE'S poems were first published in *Poetry* in 1993 and, most recently in *Euphony* (Spring 2022). A native of Pittsburgh, he has lived in New York City, Cairo, and Paris. He now makes his home in the Shenandoah Valley of Virginia.

PAUL J. PASTOR is an award-winning poet, a senior acquisitions editor for HarperCollins, and an author, most recently of *Bower Lodge: Poems*. His poetry and other writing have appeared widely, including in *The Windhover, Books & Culture, FORMA, The Los Angeles Review of Books, Presence, North American Anglican*, and *Ekstasis*, has been anthologized by *The New York Quarterly Review*, and has been featured on *The Daily Poem*. He lives in Oregon.

JESSE KEITH BUTLER lives with his wife and two children in Ottawa, Ontario. His lifelong exploration of poetic form is grounded in his experience of the life of faith: a guiding structure that opens up new possibilities for freedom.

NADINE ELLSWORTH-MORAN is an ordained minister, serving in Georgia. Through her poetry and essays, Nadine desires to engage in theological and philosophical conversations around a common table. She shares her life with her husband and four unrepentant cats.

FR. STEPHEN GREGG is a monk of the Cistercian Abbey of Our Lady of Dallas. He is a member of the English Department at the University of Dallas, and his scholarly work focuses on the poetry of Edmund Spenser.

MATTHEW CAREY SALYER is the author of two collections, *Ravage & Snare* and *Probation*, as well as a pamphlet, *Lambkin*. His work has appeared in numerous journals. He works as an associate professor at West Point and a bouncer in the Bronx.

CHRISTINA BAKER is a writer and homeschooling mother of five from Lafayette, Louisiana. She holds a B.A. in Latin and Classical Studies from Tulane University. She enjoys hiking, gardening, and identifying backyard bugs with her children.

PAUL BUSSAN is the author of four books of poetry. For more information, go to: www.amazon.com/author/paul-bussan.

LAUREN K. CARLSON is the author of the chapbook *Animals I Have Killed* (Comstock Review's Chapbook Prize 2018). Her work has recently appeared in *Crab Creek Review*, *Salamander Magazine*, *Terrain*, *The Windhover* and *Waxwing*. In 2022 she won the Levis Stipend from Friends of Writers for her manuscript in progress. Her writing has been supported by Tin House, Napa Valley Writers Conference, and Sewanee Writers Conference. Lauren currently serves as editor for *Tinderbox Poetry Journal* and holds an

MFA in poetry from the Warren Wilson MFA Program for Writers.

DANTE DI STEFANO is the author of four poetry collections, including, most recently, the book-length poem, *Midwhistle* (University of Wisconsin Press, 2023). He co-edited the anthology, *Misrepresented People* (NYQ Books, 2018). He lives in Endwell, New York.

MAX ROLAND EKSTROM holds an MFA in Creative Writing from Emerson College. His poetry appears or is forthcoming in such journals as *New American Writing, Arion*, and *U.S. Catholic*. Max lives in Vermont with his wife and three children.

MICHIAL FARMER is the author of *Imagination and Idealism in John Updike's Fiction* (Camden House, 2017) and the translator of Gabriel Marcel's *Thirst* (Cluny, 2021). His poems have appeared in *St. Katherine Review, Relief*, and *The Blue Nib*. He teaches history in Atlanta.

LADONNA FRIESEN received her M.A. in English from Missouri State University and has been teaching at Evangel University in Springfield, Missouri since 2005. She regularly reads from a collection of Kierkegaard's prayers, and one of them inspired "Burnt Sacrifice."

JOSHUA S. FULLMAN is Professor of English and Director of the University Writing Center at California Baptist University. His collection of poetry, *Voices of Iona* (2022), reflects on faith, time, and culture in the British Isles. Follow his thoughts on www.joshuasfullman.com.

DANIEL GALEF is a lapsed philosophy major and amateur artist (but prefers ink to paint). His persona poems on historical figures have appeared in *Philosophy Now, First Things*, and *Free Inquiry*, and his first book is forthcoming from Able Muse Press.

MIA SCHILLING GROGAN, an Associate Professor of English at Chestnut Hill College in Philadelphia, is a medievalist working in the areas of hagiography and women's spiritual writing. Her poems have appeared in many publications including *America, First Things*, and *Presence.*

JEFFERSON HOLDRIDGE is the author of four volumes of poetry, most recently, *The Wells of Venice* (2020). His poetry has been published in *Prairie Schooner, Poetry Ireland Review, The Irish Times, Mantis, The Anglican Theological Journal, The Quint, Honest Ulsterman,* and *Southword,* among others.

E. EDWARD HORNE lives in Virginia with his wife and children. His poems have appeared in *Taproot Magazine, Dappled Things*, and other journals.

RON HOUSSAYE'S poems have been in several literary magazines, most recently in *Moss Piglet, Sequoia Speaks,* and *Bramble.* Ron lives in Two Rivers, Wisconsin.

TRISTAN MACDONALD is a teacher of English and History at a high school in Massachusetts. He lives in North Chelmsford, Massachusetts with his wife, daughter, and son.

DAN MACISAAC writes from Vancouver Island. Brick Books published his collection, *Cries from the Ark*. His poetry received the Foley Prize from *America*, and has appeared in many journals and anthologies, including recently in *Presence* and *Poetica*'s Rosenberg Award Collection.

MARA MATTEOLI is a graduate of the University of Dallas and currently teaches at a classical elementary school. Her work has been published in *Goose River Anthology, Borrowed Solace*, and *Ever Eden*.

DANIELLE MCMAHON is a mom of two and occasional poet. Her work has appeared in *Lammergeier, Rogue Agent, swifts&slows, Fleas on the Dog*, and *Storm Cellar*, amongst others. She lives in Pennsylvania with her family.

SHARON FISH MOONEY is the author of *Bending Toward Heaven: Poems After the Art of Vincent van Gogh*, and editor of *A Rustling and Waking Within*, an ekphrastic poetry anthology, and poetry editor of *Journal of Christian Nursing*.

SEAN O'NEILL is Scottish, but has lived in the USA for the past 15 years. He is widely published in journals and has published 17 collections of poetry and the bestselling book *How To Write a Poem: A Beginner's Guide*.

MICHAEL J. ORTIZ teaches at The Heights School in Maryland. He is the author of *Swan Town: the Secret Journal of Susanna Shakespeare* (HarperCollins, 2006) and *Like the First Morning: the Morning Offering as Daily Renewal* (Ave Maria Press, 2015).

KARL PLANK, a religion scholar and poet, is the J.W. Cannon Professor of Religious Studies at Davidson College. His most recent book is *The Fact of the Cage: Reading and Redemption in David Foster Wallace's Infinite Jest* (Routledge, 2021).

LOIS ROMA-DEELEY'S poetry collections include *Like Water in the Palm of My Hand*, *The Short List of Certainties*, *High Notes*, *northSight*, and *Rules of Hunger*. She has published in numerous poetry anthologies and journals, is Associate Poetry Editor of *Presence* and is Poet Laureate of Scottsdale, Arizona.

JOYCE SCHMID'S recent poems have appeared in *New Ohio Review, The Hudson Review, Five Points, Literary Imagination*, and other journals and anthologies. A grandmother and psychotherapist, she lives in Palo Alto, California, with her husband of over half a century.

G.E. SCHWARTZ, the author of *Only Others Are: Poems, Thinking in Tongues*, and *The Very Light We Reach For*, has work published and forthcoming in *America Magazine, Dappled Things*, and *The Catholic Courier*. He lives with his family in upstate New York.

RICHARD SPILMAN is the author of *In the Night Speaking* and of a chapbook, *Suspension*. He was born and raised in Normal, Illinois, and he and his wife are raising their grandsons in Hurricane, West Virginia.

ALYSSA STADTLANDER is a writer and storyteller based in Boise, Idaho. Her work is published in *Ekstasis, Mudfish Magazine, The Windhover*, and others. For more, visit her website at www.alyssastadtlander.com.

JEANETTE W. STICKEL is a poet, speech and language therapist, and author of several children's books, including the award-winning *Mama's Needle*. Her poems have appeared in *Sojourners, Fathom, Ekstasis,* and *Spiritus*.

STUART STROMIN is a South African-American writer and filmmaker, living in Los Angeles. He was educated at Rhodes University, South Africa, the Alliance Francaise de Paris, and UCLA. His work has been published by *Jalada Africa, Immigrant Report, Nzuri, Chicken Soup for the Soul, Fiction on the Web, Macabre Ladies, The Raven, Temptation Press, The Yard, Blood Puddles, Ooligan Press, Widespread Fear of Monkeys*, and others.

ROSEANNE T. SULLIVAN is from the Boston area and currently lives in a Victorian house in San José, CA. Besides writing poetry, Sullivan writes memoir pieces, essays and articles about sacred music, liturgy, art, and whatever else captures her Catholic imagination.

TAVNER THREATT teaches twelfth-grade modern literature, as well as Dante, at Founders Classical Academy in Lewisville, Texas.

CATALINA MARGARITA UDANI is a Ph.D. candidate in Political Science at the University of Pennsylvania studying the intersection of conflict, immigration, authoritarianism, and human rights. She is also a freelance writer on global politics, an illustrator, and a photographer.

JOSEPH WALLS lives in the Ridge and Valley region of Virginia where he works as a community college English instructor. He spends much of his free time outdoors, learning again and again the simple truths we somehow always forget.

WILL WELLS'S latest full-length volumes of poetry include *Odd Lots, Scraps & Second-hand, Like New* (Grayson Books, 2017) which won the 2016 Grayson Poetry Prize and *Unsettled Accounts* (Ohio University/Swallow Press, 2010) which won the Hollis Summers Poetry Prize. "Sabbath Candles" is drawn from his current working manuscript, *Enduring Damage*, which is nearly complete.

GAIL WHITE is a contributing editor of *Light Poetry Magazine* and a frequent contributor to formalist poetry journals and anthologies, including *Nasty Women Poets, Love Poems at the Villa Nelle*, and *Killer Verse*. Her most recent books, *Asperity Street* and *Catechism*, may be found on Amazon. She lives in Breaux Bridge, Louisiana, with her husband and cats.

EDITOR BIOGRAPHIES

DANA GIOIA is an award-winning poet and critic. He has published five collections of poetry—*Daily Horoscope, The Gods of Winter, Interrogations at Noon,* which won the American Book Award, *Pity the Beautiful,* and *Meet Me at the Lighthouse.* He is also the author of several critical works, including *Can Poetry Matter?,* which was a finalist for the National Book Critics Circle Award. Gioia has worked in business, journalism, government, and education. For six years, he served as Chairman of the National Endowment for the Arts. Gioia is also the former poet laureate of California. He received the 2014 Aiken Taylor Award for lifetime contribution to American poetry. He divides his time between Los Angeles and Sonoma County, California.

MARY GRACE MANGANO is a writer and educator from New Jersey, having taught literature and composition to middle school and high school students in Chicago, New York City, and Philadelphia. As an undergraduate, she was named Senior Class Poet upon graduation, as well as the recipient of the Honorable Mention in Fiction Writing. She holds a Master's of Education from the University of Notre Dame and an MFA in Creative Writing from the University of St. Thomas in Houston, where she was the inaugural Gioia Family Fellowship recipient. Her poetry and essays have been published in *The Windhover,*

Orchards Poetry Journal, Fare Forward, Ekstasis, America, Church Life Journal, and others. She is currently working on her debut poetry collection.

ACKNOWLEDGMENTS

This book would not have been possible without the support of *Dappled Things*, especially its founder and publisher Bernardo Aparicio Garcia, Editor-in-Chief Katy Carl, and poetry editor Meredith McCann. Ann Thomas, also of *Dappled Things*, was an enormous help throughout the poetry competition, graciously answering questions, navigating organizational and online issues, and finding solutions with endless patience, expertise, and kindness.

When asked if they would be willing to sponsor the competition, Wiseblood Books immediately agreed. Their commitment and the *Dappled Things*'s large community of readers generated over two hundred submissions from across North America. Thank you to Mary R. Finnegan for her editorial support of this book and to Amanda Brown for the beautiful cover design. Joshua Hren provided equally quick and sustained support. He not only agreed to publish the anthology, but he also made room for it in the press's already crowded schedule and deftly guided the editorial process with humble prowess.

The anthology originated with Jane Harty, who felt it would realize a project her late husband had long imagined. Without her passion and devotion for this project, it might never have come to be. Because she sought to honor Ron with it, and due also to her financial support and community efforts, it is now an anthology filled with the writing of forty writers of faith who have taken up the challenge to respond to Kierkegaard—the same works to which Ron devoted much of his own writing.

We also thank *Catholic Arts Today* for the permission to publish Roseanne T. Sullivan's poem.

NOTES

1. Melville, *Moby Dick*, p. 307.

2. "Blessed Restlessness" – Kierkegaard, *Upbuilding Discourses in Various Spirits*, KW XV:218 (1847)

    "What I am seeking is not here, and for that very reason I believe it. Faith expressly signifies the deep, strong, blessed restlessness that drives the believer so that he cannot settle down at rest in this world, and therefore the person who has settled down completely at rest has also ceased to be a believer, because a believer cannot sit still as one sits with a pilgrim's staff in one's hand—a believer travels forward."

3. "Nothing But a Street-Corner Loafer" – Kierkegaard, *The Point of View*, KW XXII:61 (1849)

    "I was a street-corner loafer, an idler, a *flâneur* [lounger], a frivolous bird, a good, perhaps even brilliant pate, witty, etc.—but I completely lacked 'earnestness.' I represented the worldly mentality's irony, the enjoyment of life, the most sophisticated enjoyment of life—but of 'earnestness and positivity' there was not a trace; I was, however, tremendously interesting and pungent."

4. "Lightning Usually Strikes Churches" – Kierkegaard, *Practice in Christianity*, KW XX:247 (1850)

"... Christianity has gradually become sheer nonsense; no wonder, to recall something Luther said in one of his sermons, no wonder that 'lightning' (the fire of God's anger) 'most frequently strikes churches.' No wonder, or rather, how strange that it does not strike every Sunday in order to hit that type of preaching, which is nothing but a kind of dissoluteness, for the speaker falsely ascribes to himself and his listeners something that is not at all true of them."

5. Kierkegaard, *Either/Or*, v. 1, KW III:301 (1843)

6. Kierkegaard, *Fear and Trembling*, KW VI:115 (1843)
   "Abraham makes two movements. He makes the infinite movement of resignation and gives up Isaac, which no one can understand because it is a private venture; but next, at every moment, he makes the movement of faith. This is his consolation."

7. "My Refuge is in the Crucified One" – Kierkegaard, *Christian Discourses*, KW XVII:280 (1848)
   "—never has the need for a redeemer been clearer than when the human race crucified the Redeemer. From this moment I will no longer believe in myself; I will not let myself be deceived, as if I were better because I was not tried as were those contemporaries. No, apprehensive about myself as I have become, I will seek my refuge with him, the Crucified One. I will beseech him to save me from evil and to save me from myself. Only when saved by him and with him, only when he holds me fast, do I know that I will not betray

him. The anxiety that wants to frighten me away from him, so that I, too, could betray him, is precisely what will attach me to him; then I dare to hope that I will hold fast to him—how would I not dare to hope this when that which wants to frighten me away is what binds me to him! I will not and I cannot do it, because he moves me irresistibly; I will not inclose myself in myself with this anxiety or with this guilt consciousness that I, too, have betrayed him—I would rather, as a guilty one, belong to him redeemed."

8. "Moved by All – Yet Changed by Nothing (Prayer)" – Kierkegaard, *The Moment and Late Writings*, KW XXIII:268 (1855)

"You Changeless One, whom nothing changes! You who are changeless in love, who just for our own good do not let yourself change—would that we also might will our own well-being, let ourselves be brought up, in unconditional obedience, by your changelessness to find rest and to rest in your changelessness! You are not like a human being. If he is to maintain a mere measure of changelessness, he must not have too much that can move him and must not let himself be moved too much. But everything moves you, and in infinite love. Even what we human beings call a trifle and unmoved pass by, the sparrow's need, that moves you; what we so often scarcely pay attention to, a human sigh, that moves you, Infinite Love. But nothing changes you, you Changeless One! O you who in infinite love let yourself be moved, may this our prayer also move you to bless it so that the prayer may change the one who is praying into conformity with your changeless will, you Changeless One!"

9. Ambrose Bierce's famous definition of a Saint, found in his Devil's Dictionary (1911).

10. https://plato.stanford.edu/entries/kierkegaard/

11. https://iep.utm.edu/kierkega/#SH1a

12. https://www.masterclass.com/articles/søren-kierke-gaard-life-and-philosophy#107Vo4MLLeS8PswJ-sAHDPl

www.ingramcontent.com/pod-product-compliance
Lightning Source LLC
Chambersburg PA
CBHW071229090426
42736CB00014B/3017